The TRAVELERS COMPANION

By Elaine Schmidt

The TRAVELERS COMPANION

BY ELAINE SCHMIDT

Editor: Kent Richards

Designer: Kim Walsh

Photography: Aaron T. Leimkuehler

Illustration: Lon Eric Craven

Technical Editor: Nan Doljac

Photo Editor: Jo Ann Groves

Published by:
Kansas City Star Books
1729 Grand Blvd.
Kansas City, Missouri, USA 64108

First edition, first printing
ISBN: 978-1-61169-119-1

Printed in the United States of America by
Walsworth Publishing Co., Marceline, MO

To order copies, call StarInfo at (816) 234-4473.

KANSAS CITY STAR QUILTS
Continuing the Tradition

KansasCityStarQuilts.com

Table of Contents

Introduction

Welcome to the past! This book of projects is designed to create memorable hours shared with a young person in your life. In this age of turning to our children and grandchildren for instructions on using our smart phones and other electronics, this book offers a return to a centuries-old tradition of adults passing skills and knowledge to a younger generation. These projects, each designed to be done in a relatively short period of time, leave the teacher and learner with lovely completed works to remind them of the time spent together.

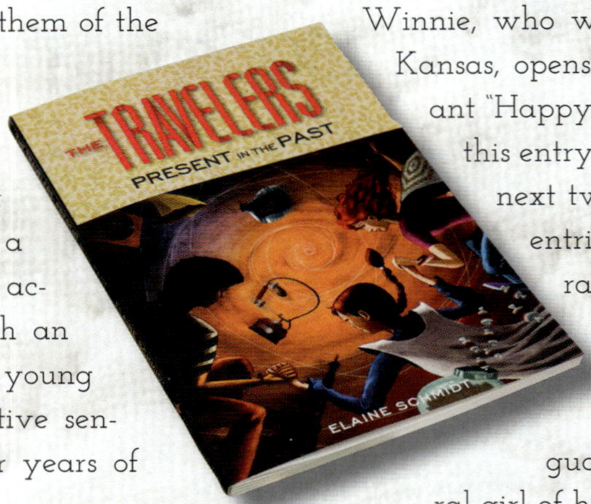

For the experienced quilter/fabric crafter, this book is not just about teaching a young person to thread a needle and stitch, although it does accomplish that. It presents you with an opportunity to share with your young project partner the skills and creative sensibilities you have developed over years of loving fabric, stitching and crafts.

Not every young person who works on these projects will become a master quilter. Regardless, they will learn some basic fabric-work skills and, perhaps most important, they will begin to appreciate the art and beauty of another person's handwork. They will also begin to appreciate the value of one-of-a-kind, handmade items.

This book is a companion to "The Travelers," a middle grade novel series that was inspired by a voice from the past. In the novels, the character of Winnie, along with her quilt and her mother's quilt, were borrowed from my husband's family tree.

The real Alice Winifred Longenecker, "Winnie," came into my life through the gift of a quilt that Winnie made for her hope chest in the 1890s.

My husband's grandmother handed me the quilt some years ago, telling me that as the only quilter in the family, it was my task to take care of the quilt and make sure it was passed on to the next generation of the family one day. Not long after that, my mother-in-law showed me a timeworn little journal that Winnie had kept in the unused, back pages of a school notebook.

Winnie, who was born in 1879 in rural Paola, Kansas, opens her first entry with an exuberant "Happy New Year to you!" The date on this entry is Jan. 1, 1895, Tuesday. Over the next two years, Winnie made sporadic entries filled with details of life in rural Paola, Kansas, in the last few years of the 19th century. She wrote with humor and spirit, in the sort of plainspoken language one would expect from a rural girl of her era. The family also has a few letters that Winnie wrote to her older sister, which are filled with the same charming writing and details of day-to-day life.

Tucked in the back of Winnie's faded journal are two brittle newspaper clippings. The two different versions of Winnie's obituary explain that she died at age 18 in a diphtheria epidemic. Winnie's journal, letters and quilt, which is the "A Little Girl's Star" variation of the Kansas City Star pattern, were tucked away by her family after her death. They have been handed carefully from one generation to the next. The combination of Winnie's engaging writing, her beautifully constructed and remarkably well-preserved quilt along with the two photographs of her that have also been handed through the generations, paint a vivid picture of a lovely girl. It's that image that inspired "The Travelers."

Winnie's journal and obituary, along with her mother's obituary, are seen against the background of her quilt.

Detail of Urilla's quilt.

About the Author

Elaine Schmidt is the author of "Hey Mom! Listen to This!: A Parent's Guide to Music" (Hal Leonard, 2010) and "All About Singing" (Hal Leonard, 2011). She has worked as a writer, arranger, translator and editor on more than 100 music publications for the Hal Leonard Corporation, G. Schirmer, and Ricordi. She lives in the Milwaukee area where she writes regularly about classical music, dance and theater for Milwaukee Journal Sentinel. Ms. Schmidt has written for Current Musicology, Back Stage, Opera Canada, Music Express, American Record Guide, Dance Teacher and other arts magazines and has scripted and hosted numerous arts broadcasts on Milwaukee Public Television. Trained as a flutist and singer, Ms. Schmidt spent more than a decade performing throughout North America before she began writing about the arts. She holds an undergraduate degree in music and an M.A. in Music Criticism.

Acknowledgements

The most important people in the creation of this book actually had nothing to do with the book itself. Their contributions were much more important. Both quilts at the center of this book, and at the center of "The Travelers" story, were passed from one generation of the Longenecker family to the next, along with the stories of the quilters who made them.

Susan Urilla Longenecker, who went by Urilla, made her quilt in 1860. More than 30 years later, she helped her teenage daughter make a quilt using some of the fabrics that had appeared in that 1860 quilt.

Urilla's quilt went to her daughter-in-law, Mamie Garrett Longenecker, who passed it on to her daughter Marjorie Longenecker Johnson. Marjorie passed it on to her son and daughter-in-law, Mark and Diane Johnson. They passed it to Mark's cousin, Judith Long Jones, after she remembered that the two quilts shared several fabrics.

Winnie's quilt, her journal and several of her letters were passed from Winnie's sister, Florence Longenecker, to her sister-in-law, Mamie Garrett Longenecker. Mamie passed the quilt to her daughter, Edith Longenecker Long, who in turn passed it to her daughter, Judith Long Jones.

My heartfelt thanks go out to the generations of the Longenecker clan who have preserved these quilts and their stories.

Thanks also to Doug Weaver, whose interest made this book possible, Kent Richards, who shaped and edited it, as well as designer Kim Walsh, photographer Aaron T. Leimkuehler, illustrator Lon Eric Craven, technical editor Nan Doljac and photo editor Jo Ann Groves for their beautiful work.

Winnie is seen here with her twin brother, Albert Maurice Longenecker, who died in 1965 at age 86.

Notes for the Experienced Project Partner

As you go through the projects in this book with a young project partner or partners, you will share not only the instruction and skills needed to complete the projects, but you will share your passion for doing handwork. Between this book and The Travelers novels, you will also share a taste of the history behind these projects and a glimpse at the generations for whom these projects were part of daily life.

In Winnie's day, the ability to sew and repair clothing and household goods was an essential skill for a rural girl. Girls began sewing at a young age, learning from their mothers, grandmothers, aunts and sisters. Some school districts taught sewing as well, as evidenced by the many sewing textbooks dating from the era.

As you help your partner learn the various techniques used in these projects, remember how foreign a needle and thread must feel in those young hands. For a taste of the strangeness of taking first stitches, and as a tension breaker, switch your own hands and give the technique a try. If you are a right-handed stitcher, switch the needle to your left hand and work several stitches. Make sure your partner sees what you're doing and shares in the humor of the results.

Good teaching is not a matter of lecturing: it's all about sharing. You are sharing your skills and knowledge, but you are also sharing yourself and your stories in a delightfully collaborative setting. The objects you create together will become treasured reminders of that time spent together. So tell your stories and your family's stories. Let your partner tell stories as well. The two of you will walk out of the sewing room sharing more than just a completed project. You'll have created a new level of shared respect and friendship as well.

I learned to stitch and crochet from my grandmother. Born in 1890, she was in her 80s when we sat at her dining room table and worked on projects together. She was patient and thorough as she explained and demonstrated the techniques I needed to know. She would fill those hours with stories from her childhood, which gave me a glimpse at her family's life at about the turn of the century, and let me see the girl she had once been. I loved those days with her at the time, but I didn't fully appreciate what a gift they were until years later. Not long ago, my mother gave me my grandmother's old sewing box, a stout, flowered cardboard box that was filled with tools and scraps. Going through it, I found a small, misshapen crocheted piece that I recognized immediately as the first bit of crocheting I did sitting at her table. Apparently she treasured those hours as well.

Each of the projects contained in the following pages are presented in three forms: beginning, intermediate and advanced. Children too young to handle needle and thread can make a crazy quilt by coloring a background and embellishing by gluing ribbon and other decorations to it. At the intermediate level, children can select and cut fabrics to fit their project, gluing it in place and gluing the embellishments as well. At the advanced level, the fabrics are stitched, by hand or machine, and the embellishments are stitched in place.

There are no age guidelines provided in the book. You know the abilities and temperaments of the children in your life and can choose the appropriate level of each of the projects in the book for each child. Whichever project and level you choose for you and your project partner, enjoy the process. Making rag-rug coasters with a child may be about the coasters for the child – for you it's about time you get to spend with that child.

Homing Pouch

The first order of business for any young Traveler is learning to make a homing pouch to prevent accidental trips to the past. In Chapter 3 of "The Travelers: Present in the Past," shortly after Nona's first accidental Travels, her grandmother makes her a homing pouch and explains that it will keep her safely in the present.

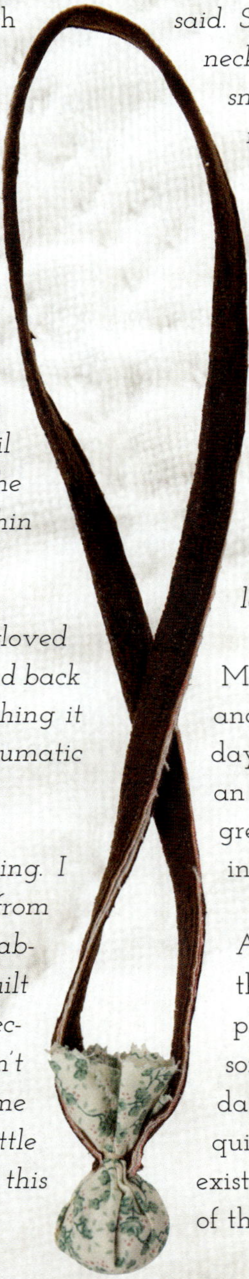

"Let's see if we can't lose those gloves," she said, wrinkling her nose at the site of Nona's hands. "I made you a homing pouch. This should keep you anchored in the present until you learn to control your Travel abilities." She held out a small fabric pouch attached to a thin strip of leather.

"What is it?" Nona asked, reaching out a gloved hand to touch it. Rethinking, she pulled her hand back and looked closely at the pouch without touching it instead. She wanted breakfast, not another traumatic trip to who knows when.

"It's a little homing pouch I made this morning. I filled it with petals from flowers that I picked from the garden this morning and a few bits of fabrics that I stitched together into a tiny, tiny quilt block. All of these things have a strong connection with this morning. The flower petals didn't exist until they opened up this morning. Same with the quilt square, since I just made it a little while ago. Even the pouch itself was made this morning."

"This will keep me from traveling?" Nona asked hopefully and a bit dubiously.

"It should do the trick to keep you in one place and time as you learn to control your abilities – at least as long as it's touching your skin," her grandmother said. She strung the leather strip around Nona's neck and decided on a good length for it. She snipped off the extra and pulled a threaded needle from the front of her shirt. She knotted the thread, stitched the loose end of the leather strip to the pouch to make a necklace of it for Nona, and then tied off the thread to hold it in place.

"There," she said, mumbling as she bit off the remaining thread from the strap. She stuck the needle in the pincushion on the table and slipped the loop over Nona's head. "Tuck that inside your shirt so it rests against your skin and, for heaven's sake, leave it there."

Most of us will never know the excitement and fear of Traveling, but we will all have days in our lives that we hate to see come to an end. Making a homing pouch can be a great way to take a little bit of a special day into the future, creating a great memento.

A homing pouch must contain several little things that are unique to a day and/or a place. A little scrap of the day's newspaper, some petals from a flower that opened that day, a little garden pebble or perhaps a bit of quilting, stitching or rug braiding that didn't exist until that day. Even the pouch itself is part of the day on which it was made.

For you and your project partner, making a homing pouch will be a simple task. You can use a little scrap from any of the items you make together, since they were created on that day.

Supplies:

- 1 - 5" to 6" circle of fabric
- 1 - 1" wide strip of faux leather - 24" long OR a 1/2" wide strip of real leather - 24" long
- Needle and thread
- Pinking shears (If you don't have pinking shears, you can clean finish the edges of the fabric circle by folding the outside edge of the circle over about a quarter of an inch and pressing it in place. Repeat the process, making another quarter-inch turn and pressing it in place. Stitch the folded fabric in place, using a sewing machine or needle and thread.)

Gather up items to place in the homing pouch, remembering that they should be specific to the day on which you're making it. Cut the leather strip and the fabric circle. You may want to have your project partner trace the circle onto the fabric, using the rim of a small plate or a cereal bowl as a template.

With fabric circle wrong-side up, assemble the pouch items in the center of the circle. Gather up the outside edges of the fabric to form the pouch around the items. Stitch the gathered fabric in place, enclosing the items, by running the needle back and forth through the gathered fabric several times, about an inch from the pinked edges. Once the pouch is gathered, wrap the thread around the outside of the gathers several times, covering the stitches you've made. Run the needle through that wrapped thread and the gathers a couple of more times. Tie it off with a sturdy knot. This should hold the items securely in the pouch and YOU securely in your time period.

If you are using faux leather, fold your 1" strip in half lengthwise and stitch as closely as possible to the raw edges. You can do this stitching by hand or by machine. If you are using a half-inch strip of real leather, there's no need to fold it over and secure it.

Using your needle and thread, attach one end of the strip to the pouch, on or near the stitching that holds the gathers in place. Fit the pouch and strap to your project partner, making sure the strap is long enough to slip easily over your partner's head. Cut off any excess strap and attach the final end to the pouch.

Susan Urilla Longenecker, who went by Urilla, made this "Sawtooth" quilt in 1860, at age 18, in Sharpsburg, Maryland. The quilt, which survived being in close proximity to "the Battle of Antietam," the bloodiest battle of the Civil War, as well as the trek to Kansas with Susan and her husband, remains in the hands of her descendants.

Urilla's Quilt

Alice Winifred "Winnie" Longenecker, daughter of Susan Urilla Longenecker, made this "Little Girl's Star" quilt in the late 1890s, in her teens. She used fabrics that are also found in the quilt her mother, Urilla, made at the same age and clearly brought along when she moved west. This quilt also remains in the hands of her family.

Winnie's Quilt

Quilting

Winnie, as I got to know her through her journal, was the inspiration for the character of Winnie in "The Travelers: Present in the Past." But the quilt she made in the late 1890s and the one her mother, Urilla, made more than 30 years earlier were the inspiration for this book. Winnie writes about her quilting, about working on her blocks and laying them out to arrange them, in her diary. What she doesn't mention is what is obvious in the quilts. Winnie's mother is clearly the person who taught her to quilt.

The three fabrics that appear in Winnie's quilt all date from the years before the Civil War. All of them appear in her mother's quilt. The quilting on Urilla's quilt is done in a feather design. Winnie's quilting is the same, with the addition of what appears to be a hand-drawn row of small feather tips. Amazingly, the pencil markings for Winnie's quilting are still visible on her quilt.

Urilla's quilt is constructed with a back-to-front handkerchief style hem instead of the binding we are so familiar with today. Winnie's was constructed in the same fashion, although with a back-to-front hem.

The other fascinating bit of history tied to Urilla's quilt is that she finished the quilt in 1860 in the town of Sharpsburg, Maryland. Two years later, Sharpsburg was the site of what remains the bloodiest battle in U.S. history, the Battle of Antietam. Her family fled and survived the battle. Winnie's "A Little Girl's Star" variation on a Kansas City Star quilt and her mother's "Sawtooth" variation on a "Kansas Trouble" quilt are a wonderful testament to the legacy of skills and artistry that were passed from one generation to the next. That tradition is the basis for every project in this book.

You are not going to make a quilt in a day with your young project partner, nor are you going to teach your partner all of the skills needed to make a quilt. But you can open his or her eyes to the tradition and fun of quilting and end the day with a completed project in hand. The experience will give your partner a taste of the art of quilting and the tradition of one generation learning from another, and the delight of working with you.

Urilla's quilt is similar to several other quilt blocks, the variations appearing in the number of small, split squares appearing on two sides of the block and the arrangement of dark and light fabrics within the block. Although the advanced project includes instruction for traditional cutting and piecing, the small, split squares can be cut and pieced in strips if you prefer.

Winnie's quilt is considered a variation on a Kansas City Star pattern. If you stare at the pattern for a bit, you may begin to see its relationship to the "Tumbling Blocks" pattern. In addition to the piecing instructions included in the advanced project, Winnie's "Little Girl's Star" quilt can also be constructed using English paper piecing, with pre-cut paper pieces that are readily available in quilt stores. It can also be constructed using foundation piecing, on foundation papers that are also readily available.

Advanced Quilting Projects

Supplies:

- **Quilt block pattern**
- **Fabric scraps or fat quarters**
- **Backing fabric the same size as the completed block**
- **One piece of fusible interfacing the same size as the completed block (if you intend to hang the finished piece on the wall)**
- **Scissors or rotary cutter and mat**
- **Sewing machine OR needle and thread for hand sewing**
- **Pillow form, or fill if finishing as a pillow**

Whether you use the patterns on pages 16 and 17 or choose a pattern of your own, remember to make the blocks large. Stitching corners and points is a challenge for a young stitcher, which is made more difficult when the project is small. Enlarging and shrinking patterns can be easily accomplished on a copier/scanner, or at a copy center.

Have your partner select fabrics for the project and iron them smooth with a steam iron.

Help your partner lay out and cut the pattern pieces. Be sure to add 1/4" seam allowance to the pattern pieces if you are doing the stitched version of the project. You may trace pieces from the patterns in the book or use a rotary cutter and ruler. Remember how dangerous a rotary cutter can be, and be sure to watch closely as your partner learns to use one.

Both quilt squares can be pieced by hand or by machine. In either case, help your partner to match up corners and points. Don't be afraid to rip out stitching and try again, if first attempts don't go well, and remember to share some of your own stitching mistake stories.

Lay out the pieces, right side up, as they will appear in the block, to check your cutting.

Urilla's Sawtooth Block Pillow

For Urilla's "Sawtooth" quilt, piece the small, half-square triangle blocks first. Create one row of five half-square triangles blocks plus one triangle and one row of four half-square triangles blocks plus one triangle. Stitch the shorter row to the smaller triangle and then stitch the longer row in place. Add the larger of the two big triangles last. See diagram 1.

diagram 1

Cut the backing fabric to match the completed block. If you are going to hang the finished block as a wall hanging, use your iron to attach the fusible interfacing to the WRONG side of the backing fabric. This added stabilizer will help the block hang flat.

Attach the backing to the completed block, with RIGHT sides together. Stitch all the way around the block, leaving several inches unstitched. Turn block right side out. If you are making a pillow, insert the pillow form or fill. If you are making a wall hanging or planning to use the block on a table or chair, press the block to smooth the seams. Hand stitch the remaining seam shut.

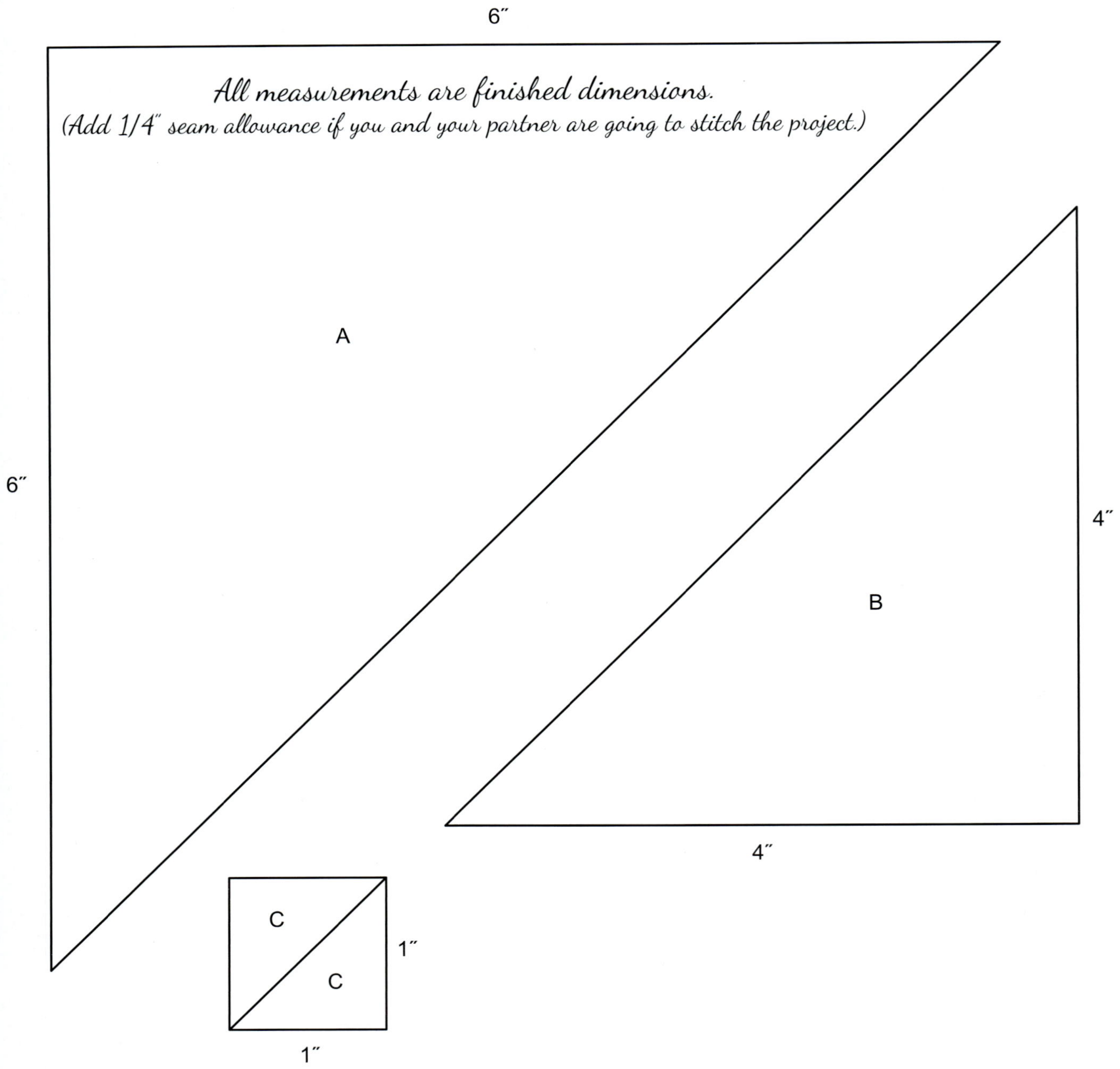

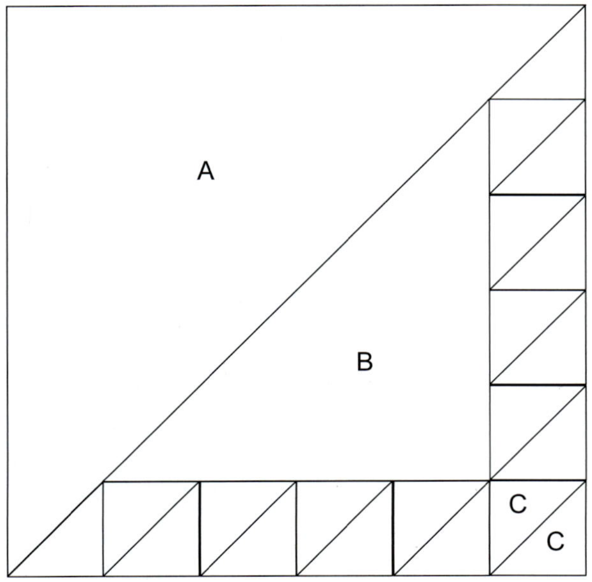

Urilla's 6″ Block

template sizes

All measurements are finished dimensions.
(Add 1/4″ seam allowance if you and your partner are going to stitch the project.)

Urilla's 15″ block templates are 1/2 scale – Enlarge 200%

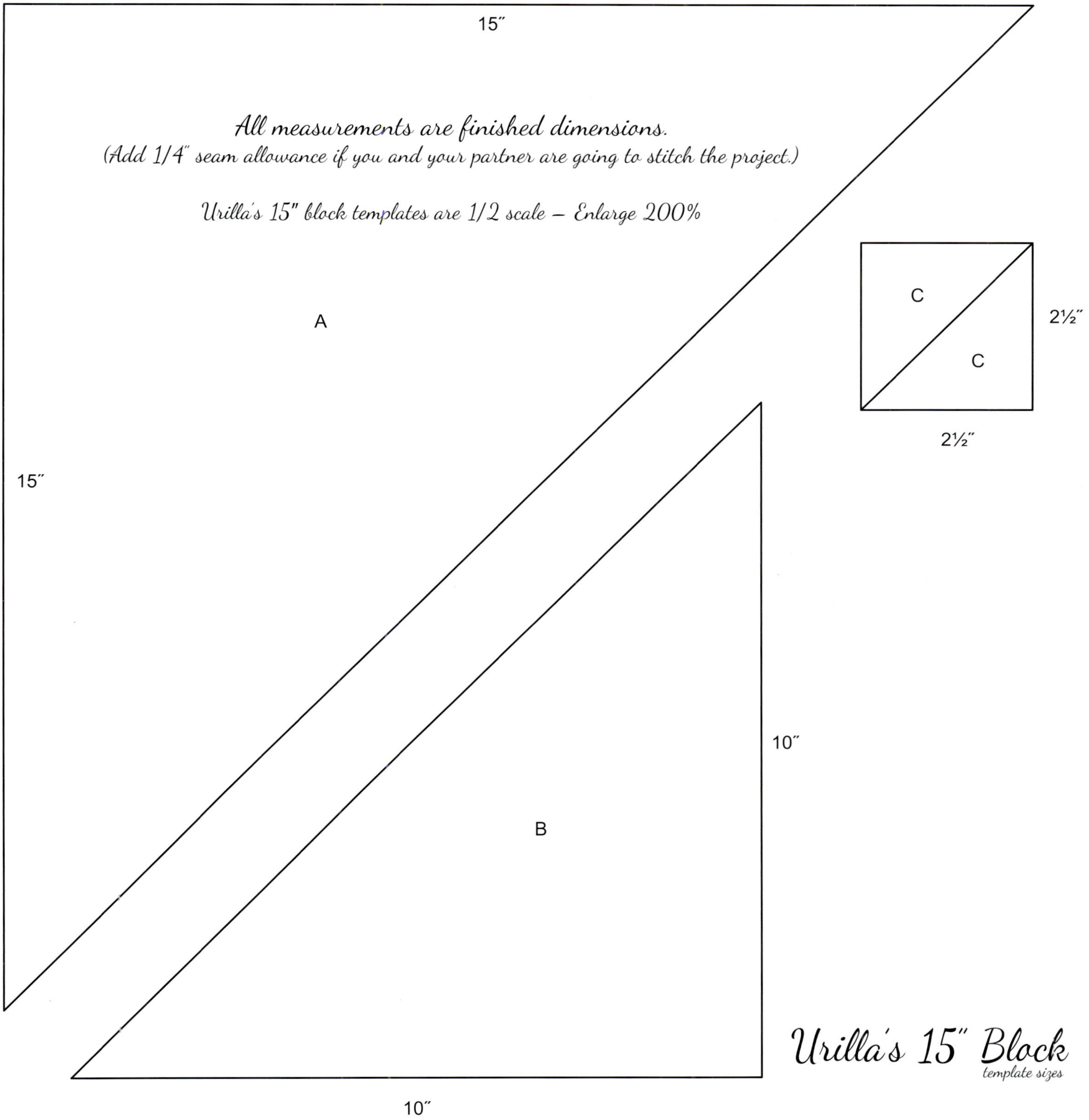

Urilla's 15″ Block
template sizes

Winnie's Little Girl's Star Block

For Winnie's "Little Girl's Star" block, piece the block as indicated – essentially creating three "Tumbling Blocks," joining them and then adding the outer diamonds. See steps 1 thru 4.

Although this project is meant to be a first experience in piecing, I have included the feather design used for both quilts in case you want to take the project to the next step and teach your project partner to do some quilting.

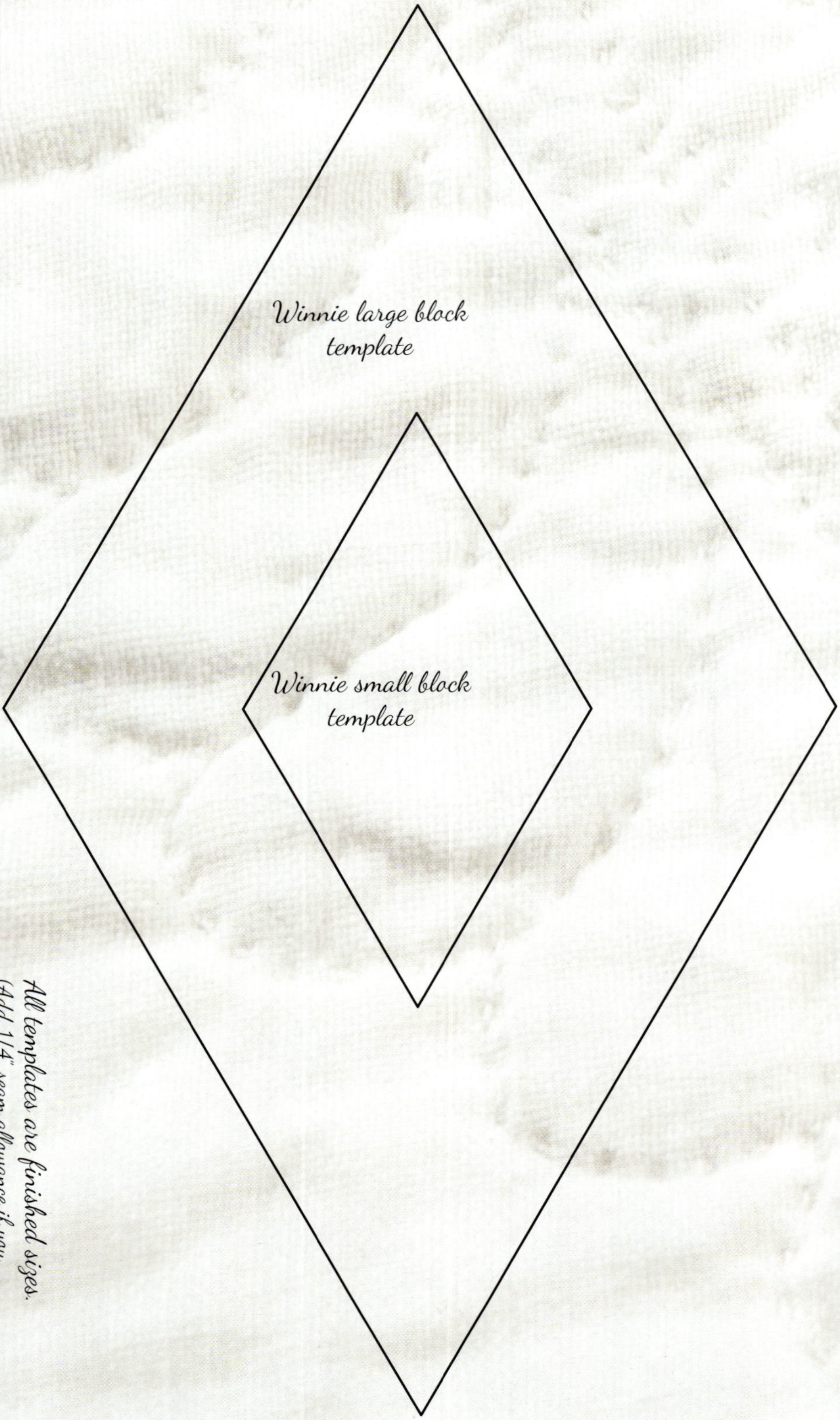

All templates are finished sizes. (Add 1/4" seam allowance if you and your partner are going to stitch the project.)

If you look closely at this detail of Winnie's "A Little Girl's Star" quilt, you can still see the pencil marks she made more than a century ago as she traced the feathered quilting design onto the fabric.

Feather quilting pattern

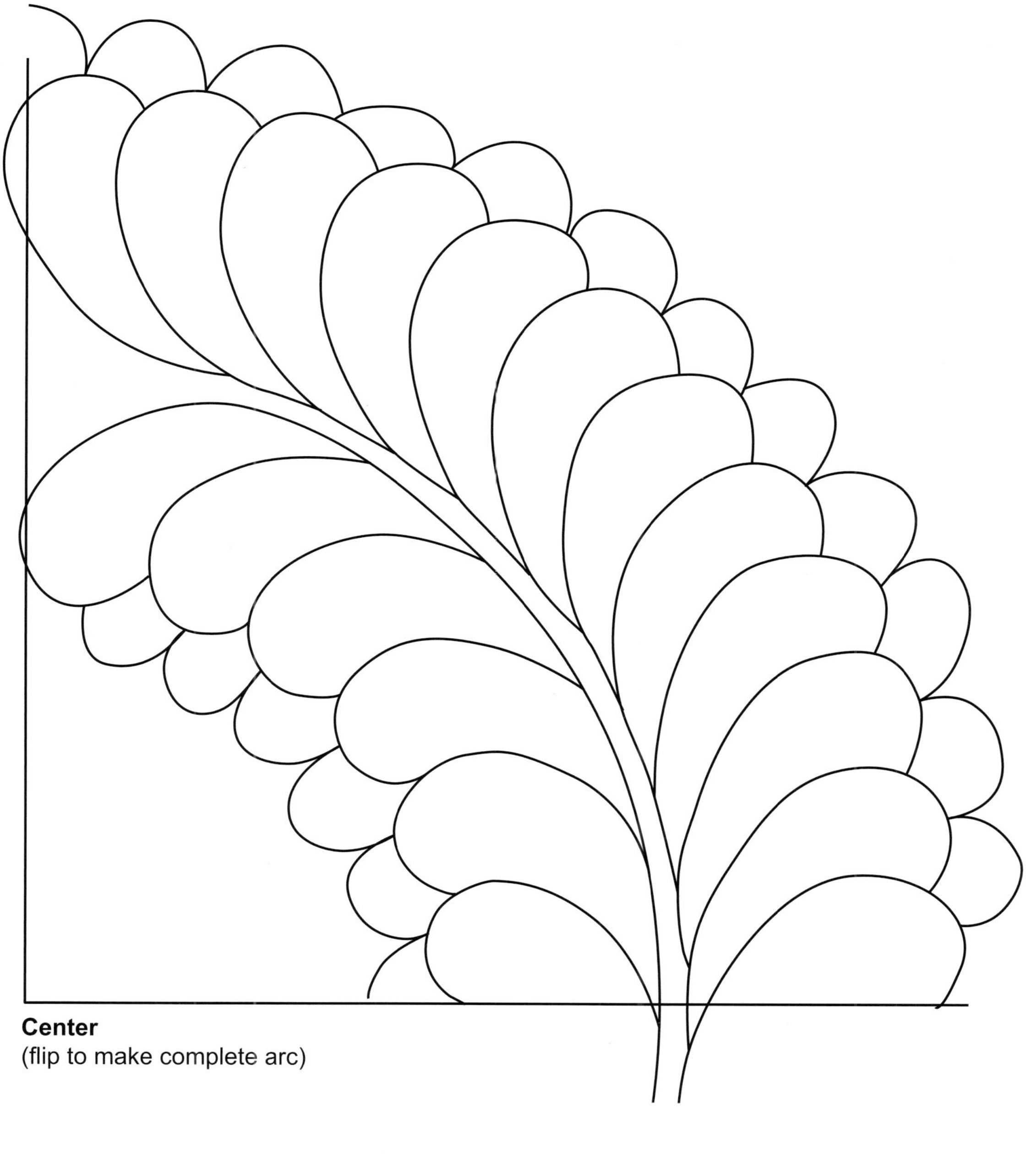

Center
(flip to make complete arc)

Intermediate Quilting

Supplies:

- Quilt block pattern
- Clear contact paper
- Fabric scraps or fat quarters
- Scissors
- A frame to fit the finished project
- A bit of backing fabric a few inches larger than the frame and of a contrasting color; it will need to serve as matting for the finished piece as well as backing.
- A permanent glue stick (I find Scotch® brand works well here.)

Let your partner choose one of the patterns on pages 16 and 17, or another pattern that you have on hand. Show the pattern to your project partner and, if possible, show your partner some examples of the pattern done in fabric. Remember that an Internet image search is a great way to find quilt photos.

Let your partner choose fabrics for the pattern from your scraps or fat quarters and iron them smooth with a steam iron. Using bits of fabric slightly larger than the pieces you will need, place them on the contact paper with the WRONG side of the fabric to the STICKY side of the contact paper. Once the fabric pieces have been backed by clear contact paper, have your project partner trace and cut pieces (no seam allowance needed) for the quilt block.

When all of the pieces are cut, assemble the block to make sure everything lines up neatly, trimming individual pieces if needed.

Cut your backing fabric to fit your frame, allowing a few inches of excess fabric overlap on each side for framing. Assemble the quilt block on the backing fabric, fabric side up. Make sure the block is centered on the fabric that will be visible in the frame.

Have your project partner glue the pieces in place on the backing fabric using the glue stick. The glue will eventually dry and adhere the pieces to the backing quite firmly. It won't happen right away, which gives the gluer some time to adjust the pieces as he or she works. When the gluing is done, the project will need to sit for 30-60 minutes as the glue begins to set. Frame the project being careful as you work; if the glue is not completely dry you could inadvertently shift some of the pieces.

Beginning Quilting

Supplies:

- **Quilt block pattern**
- **Several pieces of quilted muslin (double sided)**
- **Fabric markers**
- **Pinking shears or rotary cutter with pinking blade**
- **Sewing machine or needle and thread**

You can use the patterns provided on pages 16 and 17 for the project, or use favorite patterns of your own. The point of this simple beginning project is to introduce the fun of mixing colors in tidy, geometric quilt patterns.

Select a pattern or patterns to use for this project, remembering not to make the design too small to be colored easily by a child. Using the pinking shears, cut pieces of quilted muslin to dimensions slightly larger than the pattern you intend to use. Run a line of stitching around the outside of the muslin, about 1/4" from the edge. Trace or draw the pattern onto the muslin.

Have your project partner color the design. You might want to show your partner some fabric samples and see if he or she wants to add calico or batik details. You also might want to label the finished block with the name of the block pattern.

Remember that fabric marker is permanent, so you may want to outfit your partner in an old shirt and protect your work surface with waxed or freezer paper.

Crazy Quilting

In 1897, Winnie wrote a letter to her sister, Florence, describing a bit of the crazy quilting mania going on at the time.

"I wore that necktie to the fair, that you sent me. I think it is lovely," she wrote. "Had it on one day when I went over to Fields and Mrs. Fields had the cheek to ask me to cut a piece off for a crazy cushion she is making. I told her I wouldn't, but she insisted and tried to make me. Said it was too long any way and there was no use in putting it around twice; she wanted a piece and she was going to have it. I told her she would just have to take it out in wanting. Did you ever hear of so much cheek?"

Quilt historians trace crazy quilting to the 1876 Japanese Exhibition in Philadelphia. To this day, crazy quilters mimic "crazing," the web of fine cracks deliberately introduced to the glaze on some Japanese pots, with fine fabrics in small, random shapes. The early crazy quilting projects were sometimes known as "crazies."

Crazy quilting really took off in the U.S. in the 1880s, starting with wealthy women on the east coast. Crazy quilters were then, and still are, in constant search of snippets of special fabrics, such as silks, velvets, brocades and laces, as well as ribbons, embroidery flosses and other embellishments for their projects. Even souvenir ribbons from special events made their way into the quilts. Businesses that generated scraps of fine fabrics began selling them to crazy quilters by the bagful. Those quilters then traded scraps with each other.

The "crazies" were pieced in random, odd shapes and configurations, rather than prescribed, named patterns. Women embellished their "crazies" with yards upon yards of embroidery over every seam, and intricate bits of appliqué. Each project was a showcase for the quilter's fine handiwork and creativity. The fine fabrics and time-consuming, heavy embellishment of crazy quilting led to projects that were smaller and more decorative than bed quilts. Wall hangings, throws, pillows, samplers and small Christmas ornaments were all part of the fad.

Crazy quilting quickly made its way west into cities, towns and rural areas across the country, where fine fabrics were often replaced by cottons and more work-a-day fabric scraps to create practical versions of the quilts. But the heavily ornamented, quintessentially Victorian crazy quilts of the era remained the ideal.

Part of the fun of making a crazy quilt project with a young partner is the process of turning leftovers and stray items into art. Speak to your partner a few weeks ahead of project day and explain what materials you'll be using. Let him or her start collecting items. In the Beginning and Intermediate projects, anything that can be glued in place is fair game.

Crazy quilt from the collection of Carol Warwick Jacobson,
Whitefish Bay, Wisconsin, on gracious loan from her daughter, Heidi Knudsen.

Advanced Crazy Quilting

Supplies:

- A selection of fancy fabric scraps
- An assortment of beads, buttons and scraps of ribbon and trim that can be stitched to fabric
- Sewing machine or needle and thread
- Pinking shears or rotary cutter with pinking blade
- A small-to-medium sized frame to hold the completed work

Keep this project small. Your project partner will be stitching seams, either by hand or machine, and will be hand-stitching embellishments in place once the piecing is done. By keeping the project small, you will be able to complete it in a day, and reduce stress and frustration while it is in progress.

Collect fabrics, trims and embellishments for the project. You may want to make a trip to a fabric and/or craft store with your partner for this project and shop the clearances on fabric and trim. Remember that you will only need tiny bits of fabrics, probably less than a 4" square of any fabric you include.

Pink the edges of the fabric pieces as you get ready to use them to prevent fraying.

You and your partner have a choice between hand sewing the fabrics together or using a sewing machine. If you're going to hand stitch the pieces together, use a backstitch. (Instructions on page 42.) Normally, quilters make a 1/4" seam as they piece, but for a first crazy quilting project, it won't matter if your partner makes a deeper seam. A deeper seam may make the fabric and needle easier for your partner to control.

Have the frame handy as you and your partner are working, remembering to place your best and favorite fabrics prominently in the crazy quilted piece as it will appear in the frame.

When the pieces are stitched together, you can steam it VERY LIGHTLY with a steam iron. Take care to cover the piece with a piece of cotton fabric or dishtowel. Keep the iron just above the protective fabric and apply steam. Pressing the iron down onto the fabric will mash the velvet you might have used and may melt or burn some of the other fabrics.

Selecting and applying the embellishments will take a while. Embellishments should be hand stitched to the crazy quilt. You can help your partner learn a few decorative crazy quilt stitches if you like (there are instructions for dozens available online), but applying premade embellishments makes it far more likely that your project will be done in a day.

Fit the piece into its frame, and sit back to enjoy the handiwork.

Intermediate Crazy Quilting

Supplies:

- **One piece of poster board, 12" x 14" or smaller (Choose a bright color because it will serve as a frame for the completed project.)**
- **A selection of fancy fabric scraps**
- **An assortment of beads, buttons and scraps of ribbon and trim that can be glued to fabric**
- **A pencil**
- **A permanent glue stick**
- **Elmer's Glue-All®**
- **Pinking shears or rotary cutter with pinking blade**

Draw a pencil line about 1 1/2" from the outside of the piece of poster board, explaining that by keeping the fabric and trim inside this line, the poster board becomes the project's frame.

Cut and fit pieces of fabric to the poster board, taking time to arrange the entire piece before beginning to glue the pieces of fabric in place. Using the glue stick, apply several swipes of glue to the fabric and/or the poster board to secure the fabric pieces in place.

Once the fabric is in place, it's time to start applying embellishments with Elmer's Glue-All®. Be sure to use plenty of glue. What looks like a big blob of glue seeping under or through the embellishments will be nearly invisible when it's dry and will hold the embellishments firmly in place.

Leave the piece sitting flat until the glue has completely dried, at which point you can hang the piece on a wall. If you decide to frame it, the exposed poster board will serve as a mat inside the frame.

Beginning Crazy Quilting

Supplies:

- 1 - 8" to 10" square, circle or rectangle of quilted muslin (double sided)
- Fabric markers
- Pinking shears or rotary cutter with pinking blade
- An assortment of beads, buttons and scraps of ribbon and trim that can be glued to fabric
- Elmer's Glue-All®
- Sewing machine or needle and thread

Cut the quilted muslin to whatever size and shape you would like the finished project to be. Keep it under 10' square (or round) to keep the project manageable and to make it easier to hang when it is completed. Run a line of machine or hand stitching about a 1/4" from the outside of the piece to prevent fraying.

Using a fabric marker, draw some lines on the fabric to simulate the random shapes of fabric pieces in a crazy quilt. Let your project partner color the shapes with fabric marker. Remember that fabric marker is permanent, so you may want to outfit your partner in an old shirt and protect your work surface with waxed or freezer paper.

Once the shapes are colored, it's time to select and apply embellishments. These will be glued in place with Elmer's Glue-All®. Make sure to use plenty of glue. What looks like a big blob of glue seeping under or through the embellishments will be nearly invisible when it's dry and will hold the embellishments firmly in place.

Leave the piece sitting flat until the glue has completely dried, at which point you can frame it or hang it on a wall. Glue or stitch a loop of ribbon to the back of the piece to hang it.

Rug Braiding

Winnie wrote several entries in her journal about tearing rags for rugs or about working on rugs with her mother. On Sunday, Jan. 11, 1895, she wrote, "This afternoon Ma and I tore and sewed carpet rags and churned. We have about 24 pounds sewed."

Winnie grew up on a farm near Paola, Kansas. American farm life in the 1890s, when she was writing her journal, was a frugal, do-it-yourself lifestyle. Nothing was wasted and nothing was thrown away until the family had gotten as much use out of it as possible. Rag rugs are a great example of using every scrap again and again.

Salvageable fabric from old sheets, nightgowns and nightshirts, aprons and so on was torn into narrow strips and rolled into balls or ovals. In her journal she writes about how many "pounds" they have torn and sewed. Fabric requirements for rugs were gauged in pounds, rather than in yards, in those days and are still occasionally referred to that way today. A pound of fabric works out to between 3 and 4 yards, depending on the weight and width of the fabric. I usually use an estimate of 3 1/2 yards. Since women and girls of Winnie's time would have gotten as much wear as possible out of the fabric goods in their lives and would never have considered buying new fabric to be torn up for rugs, it could take several years for them to amass enough fabric strips to make a good-sized rug.

When those completed rugs began to wear out, or were stained or burned by fireplace embers, the damaged portions were cut out and the remainders were mended and reused. They might turn up as hot pads, foot warmers in a buggy, or a pad used when storing a saddle on a wooden board in a barn.

In Winnie's time there were three main methods for making rugs: braiding, crocheting and nålbinding (also known as toothbrush rugs because the needle used to make the rugs was crafted from the handle of a worn-out toothbrush). Braiding is the most straightforward of these methods to teach to children, particularly young children.

Although Winnie and her mother would never have dreamt of buying new fabric for rag rugs, you might want to consider it. You don't need beautiful fabric for rugs, nor do you need the best quality fabric. Discount department stores sell overstock and out-of-season fabric for as little as $1 per yard several times each year. If you purchase this low-end fabric for a rug project, just make sure that fabric on the bolt is not fraying excessively, which means it will fray badly while you work with it and after the projects are done.

Braiding General Directions

Strip Preparations:
You can either cut or tear your fabric into 2" strips, although tearing is much quicker and is a bit of giddy fun for a young child. To tear, simply make little cuts at 2" intervals on the selvedge of the fabric. Then you and your partner each grab the fabric on opposite sides of a snip and pull.

Connecting Strips:
As you work on these braided items, you will have to join strips of fabric together. You can sew the ends together as you braid, but that requires stopping and pinning the last crossover of the braid to keep it from loosening up. The best method for joining strips is also the simplest method and will be more fun for your project partner than having to stop to sew the ends. To join two strips, cut a 1/2" long lengthwise slit about an inch from both ends of each strip. See step 1. Line up one slit from one strip and one from the other, with the length of the strips extending off in opposite directions. See step 2. Take the free end of the top strip and bring it through the two slits from the bottom. See step 3. Pull it through to form a compact knot that joins the two lengths together. See steps 4 and 5. Pay attention to how much length you have left on all three braiding strips as you work, taking care not to let two or three joining knots line up in the same place on the braid. That will make a thick, hard lump in your finished project. Do not fasten all of the strips together before you begin braiding. To avoid nasty tangles attach them one at a time, as you come to the end of a braided strip.

Braiding:
The following simple steps will make your braiding projects easy to handle. To begin, stitch one end of each of three strips of fabric together and pin or otherwise anchor the stitched ends to a mattress or piece or upholstered furniture. As the braid begins to grow in length, you will find yourself backing away from the bed or furniture in order to keep working. You may either re-pin the strip, anchoring it closer to where you're braiding as needed. To save time, you may also use a door or window to secure the braid. Simply open the door or window and close it on the already completed braid, close to where you're working. Open the window or door and reposition the braid as needed – it's quicker than pinning and unpinning. If you're using a door, you may have to press your foot against the bottom of the door to keep the braid secured.

Start braiding by crossing one of the outside strips over the strip next to it and then doing the same with the opposite outside strip. Continue in this fashion, always alternating strips, until the braid is 4" or 5" long. Running a hand along the length of one of the strips after every third or fourth crossover will help prevent tangles in the loose ends of the strips. See steps 1 thru 5. Your braid should be snug, but not excessively tight, or the finished piece will curl. If your project partner has difficulty with the braiding at first, you will be able to undo the braid quite easily and have him or her begin again.

Working with a partner will also save a tremendous amount of time. As the person braiding nears the end of one of the strips of fabric, the other person can get the next strip ready. This saves having to pin the ends of the braid in order to knot the strip in place. Taking turns at both tasks will prevent either of you from getting stiff and sore and will give a great feeling of teamwork to the project.

Here you will find three projects based on rug braiding. The fobs in the Beginning project can be used on key chains or attached to handbag handles, suitcases or backpack zipper pulls as decoration – or pretty much anywhere you might like a little hand-made decoration. The coasters and trivets are intended for everyday use.

Connecting Strips:

Step 1 *Step 2* *Step 3* *Step 4* *Step 5*

Braiding:

Step 1 *Step 2* *Step 3* *Step 4* *Step 5*

Braiding Projects

The Intermediate and Advanced versions of the braiding project are quite similar. They both entail making coasters and trivets, but they employ different methods of finishing the items. In the Intermediate project, the braids are glued in place, while in the advanced projects they are stitched in place.

Making rag rugs (coasters or trivets too) is a matter of starting with the end of a braid and making a round or oval shape by wrapping the braid around and around in a coil. When the object has reached the size you intended, simply cut off the braid, fold under the last bit of braid and anchor securely.

Photos 1

Photos 2

Advanced - Set of Four Coasters

Supplies:

- **Three strips of fabric 2" x 1 1/2 yards each of different fabric for each coaster**
- **Five large safety pins**
- **Sewing machine or needle and thread**
- **One long hand-sewing needle**
- **Stout thread (preferably quilting thread) in a color that will not stand out against the fabric of your braid**

Begin by tearing and braiding your fabric using the methods described in the General Directions. When you are done with your braids, move to a table and begin coiling one of the braids to form a coaster. Place the narrow sides of your braid together and the broader side flat on the table as you coil and stitch through the braid from one layer of the coil to the previous layer. See photos 1 and 2. Take a stitch every 1/2". When you reach the end of the braid, turn the raw edges under and secure.

Trivet:

Follow the instructions above using strips 4 yards long for 1 - 9" stitched trivet. Follow the stitching instructions above to make the trivet.

Intermediate - Set of Four Coasters

Supplies:

- **Three strips of fabric 2" x 2 yards each of different fabric for each coaster**
- **Five large safety pins**
- **Sewing machine or needle and thread**
- **Elmers Glue-All®**
- **One large piece of waxed paper or freezer paper**

Begin by tearing your fabric into strips using the method described in the General Directions. Using a sewing machine or needle and thread, create the beginning point for your braid by sewing the 3 strips together at one end. Insert a safety pin through the joined ends and pin to a mattress or couch.

Once you reach the end of the strips, use the sewing machine or needle and thread to secure the end of the braid by stitching through all of the layers of strips several times. Repeat the process three times to make 4 coasters.

Continues on page 37

Once you have your braids done, it's time to move to a table and break out the glue. Spread the piece of waxed paper or freezer paper on the table to protect it from the glue. If you were going to stitch the coils in place, as instructed in the advanced section, you would lay the braid flat on the table as you coil. Since you are going to glue the braids in place, you will need to stand the braid on its narrow side, thus exposing the greatest surface of the braid to glue. Apply a generous amount of glue to both faces of the braids you're securing. See photo. Continue coiling until you reach the end of the braid. Fold the raw edges of the end under themselves and glue in place. Use one of the pins to secure the end, pinning through as many layers of braid as the pin will hold. Repeat this process for the other 3 coasters.

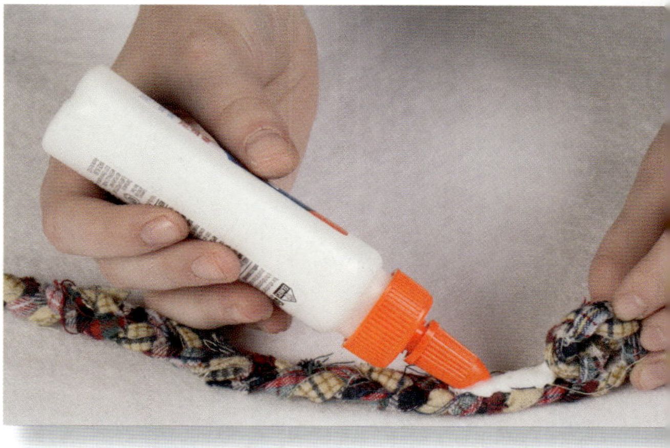

Dab off any excess glue that you can see on both sides of the glued coaster or trivet. Leave the coasters on the waxed paper overnight or until they have dried.

Trivet:

Follow the instructions above using strips 5 yards long for 1 - 9" glued trivet.

Note: Elmer's Glue-All® is not the same as Elmer's School Glue®. It is far more durable than the School Glue, but is still non-toxic. The glued coasters were unaffected by being submerged in water for several minutes and were also unaffected by the heat of a mug filled with a hot beverage.

Beginning - Short Fob

Supplies:

- **One large key ring**
- **Three fabric strips, each 2" x 1 1/3 yards**
- **Pinking shears**
- **Two large safety pins**
- **Sewing machine or needle and thread**

For this project, you will want to pink all of the edges of the fabric strips after tearing, to prevent the finished item from fraying. Tip: You can buy a pinking blade for your rotary cutter. Using that blade to cut your strips will give you strips that are already pinked and ready to go.

Pin the key ring to a piece of upholstered furniture or a mattress. Feed all three strips through the key ring, letting them hang from the ring. Even up the loose ends so that the key ring is at the midpoint of each strip. This should give you 6 strips of fabric hanging from the key ring. Two strips of each color.

Working the 6 strips in pairs (match the identical fabrics), help your project partner to braid. Once the braided portion of the fob is completed, use the sewing machine or needle and thread to secure the end of the braid by stitching through all of the layers of strips several times. You've just created a key fob.

Long Fob:

Follow the instructions above using strips 2 yards long and make the braid 8" or 9"long.

Redwork

Winnie refers to her sewing several times in her entries, but never specifically mentions redwork. Given the popularity of redwork during her childhood, she undoubtedly saw quite a bit of it and most likely did some redwork herself. The simple, one-color embroidery was taught to girls as young as 8 years old in Winnie's day.

In many ways, redwork is the opposite of crazy quilting. Although they both became popular in America in the second half of the 19th century, they initially appealed to different groups of women. Crazy quilting began among relatively wealthy urban women and required fine fabrics and lots of fancy embroidery stitches, while redwork became popular among women who had neither the time nor the money to make elaborate, heavily embellished items that were far more decorative than practical. Redwork, featuring line drawings outlined in simple stitches on a plain, white, cotton background, was an inexpensive form of needle art and was quick to complete.

One of the great delights of redwork remains the fact that most patterns require just a few basic, easy to remember stitches: the backstitch (or the similar stem stitch) and the French knot. The red-on-white color scheme is eye-catching and somehow merry. Although red was, and still is, the most popular choice for this style of embroidery, it is also done in blue thread on a white background and called – you guessed it – bluework. You and your project partner can obviously choose any color you like.

Redwork began to appear in the middle of the 1800s, in Europe and in the U.S. Prior to about 1840, red was a bit of a frightening proposition to most quilters and stitchers. Most red dyes available at the time faded quickly to dingy, pale brown or bled, spreading color to other fabrics and even to the skin of someone wearing red clothing. But thanks to a dying process that emerged from the Middle East in the middle of the century, a colorfast red color suddenly became practical in fabrics and in threads. Knowing that it wouldn't bleed when washed, quilters and stitchers sought out fabric, floss and cotton embroidery thread in this "Turkey Red."

Patterns for redwork were once sold preprinted on white cotton squares, as well as on paper, requiring tracing onto fabric. Traceable and heat-transfer patterns are most common today. The inexpensive, preprinted squares were known, at least for a short time, as "penny squares" and are often referred to that way today. Penny squares could be completed, framed and hung on a wall. They could be stitched together to create a coverlet or quilt. The patterns could be traced onto table linens, aprons, pillowcases, children's clothing, handkerchiefs and a host of other items. Completed penny squares could also be appliquéd onto those larger items.

Redwork remains popular for the same reasons it was popular more than a century ago – it's inexpensive to do and the projects can be completed relatively quickly. A quick Internet image search for "redwork" will prove that point rather quickly. The same search for "bluework" also yields quite a bit. Websites, blogs and books are devoted to the topic, so if you are really bitten by the redwork bug, you won't be alone. The advantage you have over previous generations of redworkers is the bevy of redwork-able line drawings available on the Web. Most printers or copiers can enlarge or reduce any line drawing to the size of your choice.

Redwork "Penny Squares" stitched by my grandmother, Helen Burdorf Eggold, who was born in Nebraska in 1890, when Winnie was 11 years old.

Advanced Redwork

Supplies:

- One piece of white or off-white fabric large enough to hold the design and to facilitate framing
- One additional piece of white or off-white fabric the same dimensions as the one on which you will trace your pattern
- Pinking shears or rotary cutter with pinking blade
- One fine red marking pen or pencil
- One line drawing design
- One small to medium embroidery hoop (optional)
- Needle and thread for basting two layers of fabric
- Embroidery needles, size 9
- Needle threader
- Embroidery floss or cotton embroidery thread (see instructions for considerations)
- Embroidery or other fine scissors
- One thimble
- One frame or embroidery hoop large enough to display complete design

The patterns presented in this section are taken from illustrations found in "Samplers and Stitches: A Handbook of the Embroiderers Art," by Mrs. Archibald Christie, published in 1921. The illustrations were created by the author. See page 48.

Several of the redwork patterns are small enough that a young stitcher with a little needle experience should be able to complete one in a couple of hours. Using pinking shears, cut a piece of fabric for the embroidery, making sure to leave 4" or 5" of excess fabric on all sides of the design. Have your partner trace the design onto the fabric using the fine marking pen or pencil. A light board will work well but so will taping the design to a window and taping the fabric over it.

Cut a piece of the same fabric in the same dimensions as the first piece to use as a stabilizer for the project. Place the stabilizer beneath the fabric on which you have traced the design, matching the corners and edges, and baste the two together. The stabilizer will keep the fabric from stretching and will help hide the knots and crossovers of floss that might show through from the back to the front of a single layer of fabric.

Look over the design and make sure you know what stitches are going to be used. The designs included in this book require a backstitch (or the related stem stitch) and a French knot. Following the instructions below, help your project partner learn and get comfortable with the stitches using a test piece of fabric. This is also a good time to decide if using a hoop will make the stitching more or less comfortable.

Note:
Some redworkers like to use two strands of embroidery floss for their projects; others prefer one strand of cotton embroidery thread. I prefer the single strand, as it avoids tangles and makes a strong, smooth stitch. The single strand is also easier to thread through the eye of the needle than two strands of floss, even if you use a threader. The rich red of DMC # 498, sold in a ball, not as looped strands, is my favorite color. It is readily available at craft and fabric stores.

Backstitch

The backstitch is the handiest, most essential stitch you will ever learn or teach. When applied to a single layer of fabric, it makes a beautiful, even outline stitch that will resist snagging and puckering. It is also the best stitch to use when stitching a seam, joining two pieces of fabric. When you have to do a hand-repair on a seam in anything from a pair of pants to draperies or a tent, this is the best stitch to use. When the backstitch is done well, it can be almost impossible to tell from the exterior of a garment if the seam was sewn by hand or machine. You will use the backstitch in a decorative application here and in a functional application in the crazy quilting section of the book.

Make sure your project partner has a chance to practice the stitches before moving to traced patterns. To do this, take a bit of fabric, and draw a simple line or shape on it with the fine red pen or pencil.

Cut a double strand of floss or a single strand of embroidery thread no more than 2 feet long. Thread your needle (using the threader if using two strands of floss) and make a single knot in the end of the thread farthest from the needle.

Bring the needle up through the fabric on the line you are about to stitch, 1/8" to 1/4" from the beginning of that line. Pull your thread through, until the knot is touching the back side of the fabric. Moving the needle back to the beginning of the line, poke your needle into the fabric at the starting point of the line and back through to the top 1/8" to 1/4" from where you began. Pull the needle and thread through until the thread is snug. Move the needle back to the end of that first stitch and poke it through the hole that ended the first stitch, bringing it back up 1/8" to 1/4" from where you last came up through the fabric. Pull the thread through until it is snug. Repeat this stitch, always going back down through your previous stitch, to the end of the line. By doubling back on each stitch, you create a secure, stable line of stitching. When you're nearing the end of the thread, knot it off on the back side of the fabric and begin a new thread.

French Knot

Thread your needle with a double strand of floss or single strand of embroidery thread, no more than 2 feet long. Knot one end. Bring the needle up from the back of the fabric at the spot on which you want to make a French knot. Pull it through until the knot touches the back of the fabric. Grasp the thread near the fabric and wrap it around the sharp end of the needle three times. Holding the thread in place with your thumb, insert the needle into the fabric beside where you came up. Pull the needle and thread through slowly, holding onto the thread with your thumb until the last possible moment. Either move on to the next knot or to another bit of stitching without cutting the thread, or knot it and cut it off on the backside of the fabric if you're done.

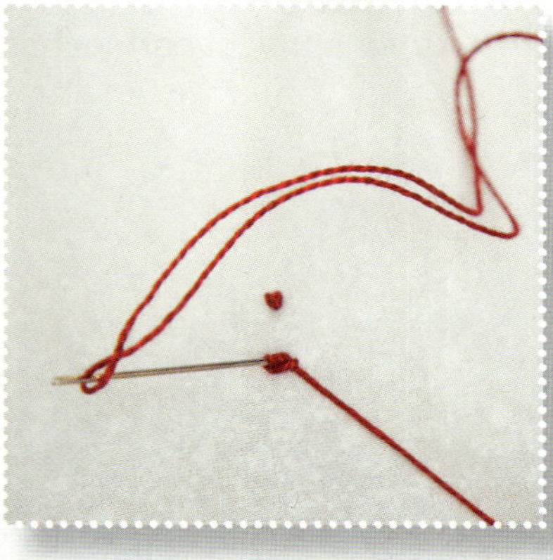

When the redwork project is done, use a pressing cloth and press the finished piece of redwork gently, with a steam iron, to remove any wrinkles. You can frame the completed redwork in a traditional picture frame, with or without protective glass. Many people opt for no glass, so that the texture of the work is visible. To frame a completed redwork project in an embroidery hoop, center the redwork image in the hoop and make sure there are no puckers or slack sections on the surface of the fabric. Cinch the hoop tightly. Trim the excess fabric with pinking shears so that there is no more than 2" or 2 1/2" of fabric outside the hoop. Run a hot steam iron along the back side of the hoop, pushing the loose fabric into the hoop, toward the backside of the embroidery. You can secure the loose corners in large, criss-crossed basting stitches (using white thread) if you like, but if you get a crisp crease along the edge of the hoop, you shouldn't need to anchor the fabric. DO NOT press the fabric against the hoop if you're using a plastic hoop as a frame! You may dress up the hoop with a bow made of red ribbon, lace or fabric.

Intermediate Redwork

Supplies:

- One fairly simple redwork pattern or line drawing
- Enough red yarn to outline the pattern in yarn
- One piece of white or off-white muslin large enough to contain the design you choose, with 4" to 5" of excess fabric around the pattern to facilitate framing
- Pinking shears or rotary cutter with pinking blade
- One fine red marking pencil or pen
- One bottle of Elmer's® all-purpose glue
- One frame without protective glass OR an embroidery hoop large enough to hold the completed image
- A piece of waxed paper or waxed freezer paper slightly larger than the project

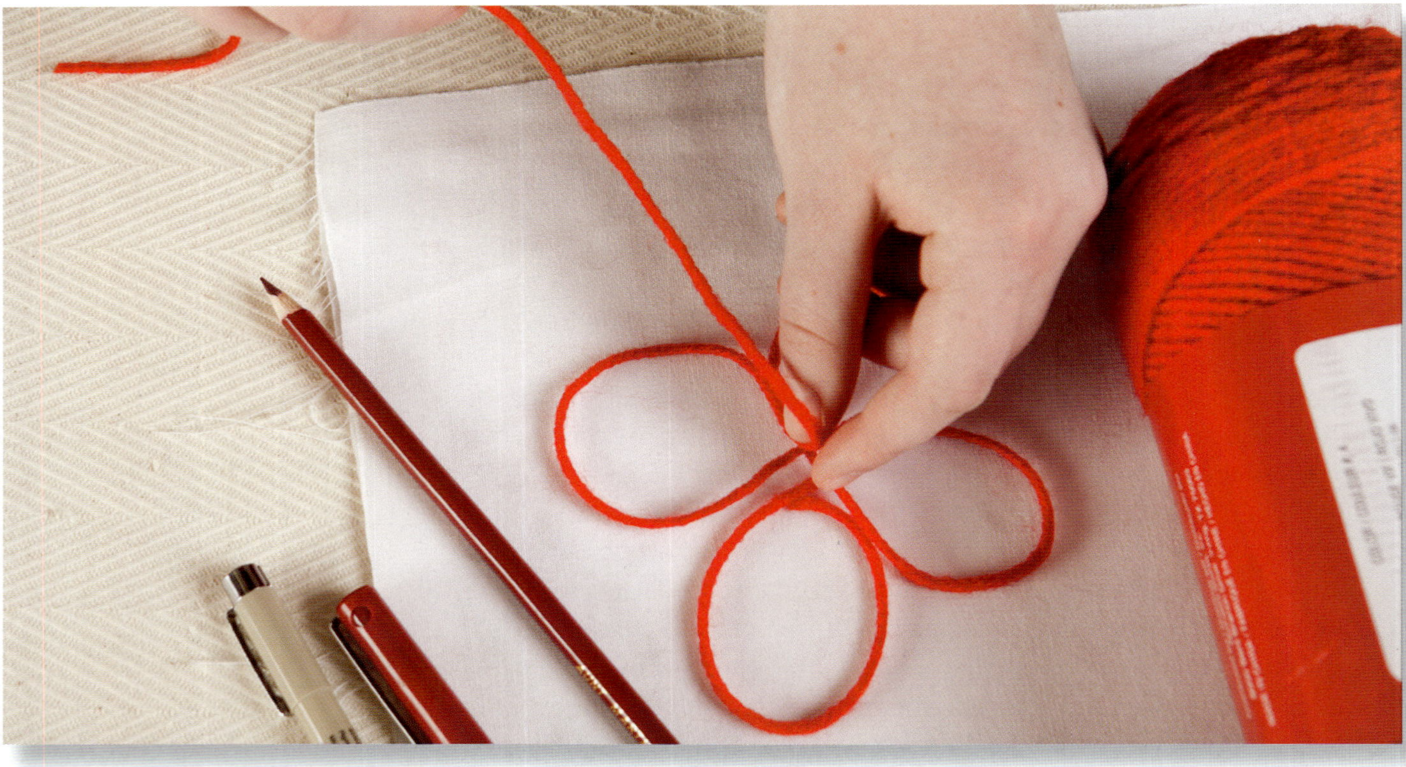

In this project, you and your partner will glue strands of yarn onto the lines of the line drawing. You might want to do a couple of test runs on paper, using simple shapes, to give your partner a chance to get used to the process.

Using pinking shears, cut your fabric, leaving a few inches beyond what will be visible in whatever type of frame you've chosen. Center the pattern on the fabric, and trace with your red marking pencil or pen. Use a light board to make the image clearly visible, or tape the pattern to a window and then tape the fabric over the image.

If you and your project partner have a specific image in mind for your project, a Christmas tree or Valentine's heart for instance, you can certainly draw your own pattern or do an Internet image search. Enter the name of the image and the words "line drawing" and click on your browser's image search icon. Print the image, trace it onto fabric and have fun. Children's coloring books can also provide a great source of redwork images for children.

It would be good to have a redwork project of your own to work on while your partner is working on his or hers. Start with a test project of simple shapes and lines, explaining that it works best to work with short bits of yarn, rather than long strands. Have your partner trace a small section (3" or so) of the pattern's lines in glue, and then place strands of yarn on the glue and press them gently into place. Always work on a sheet of waxed paper, or on the waxed side of a sheet of freezer paper. Although a long, uncut strand of yarn will make a smoother line than several short pieces, it is also likely to be pulled out of the glue by young hands, causing frustration and getting glue and yarn fuzz on the white fabric. Unlike paper, fabric won't pucker from the moisture of the glue. When the project is finished, leave it sitting on the waxed paper to dry. Once it's completely set (the glue will go from a thick, milky white liquid to a nearly clear, hard substance), simply peel the waxy paper from the back of the project. Place in frame or hoop.

Redwork templates

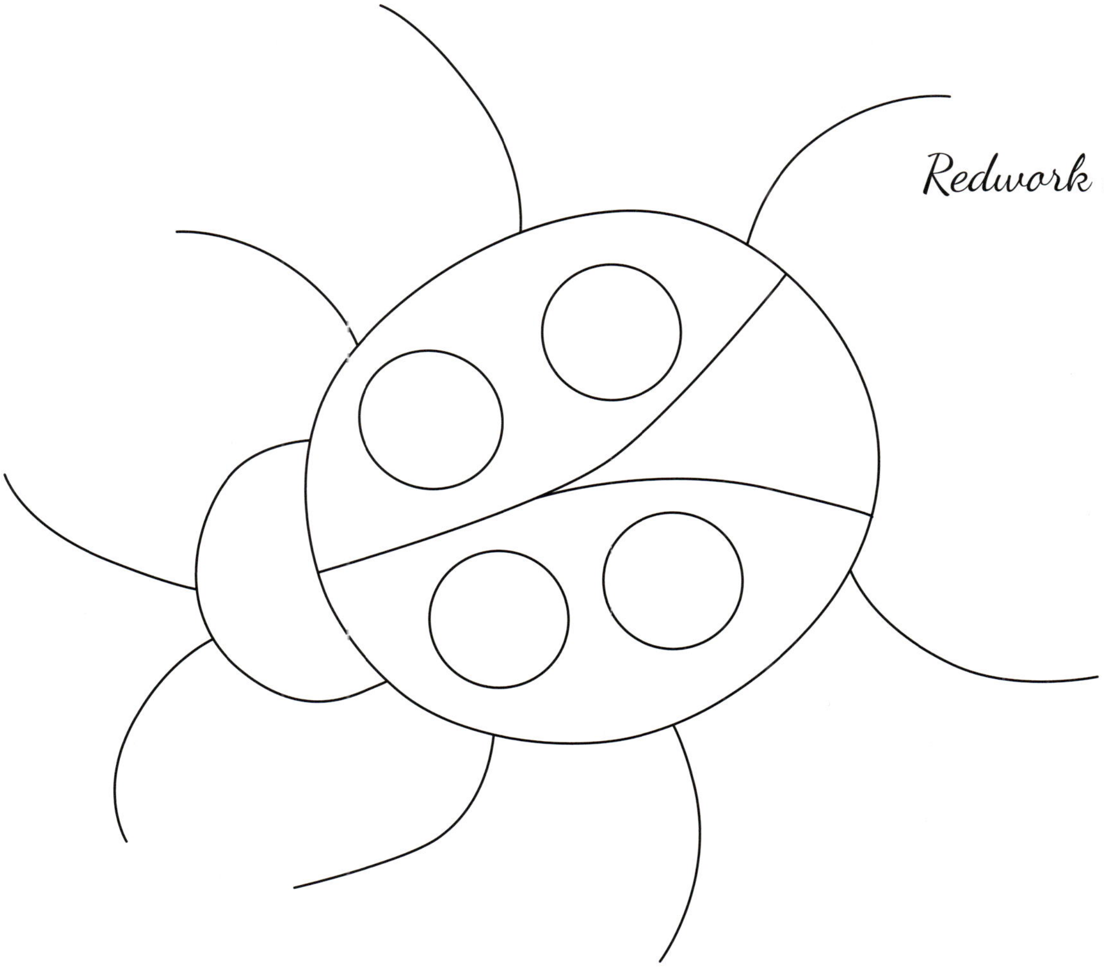

Beginning Redwork

Redwork templates

Supplies:

- One piece of quilted muslin – fabric on both sides
- One line-drawing image that you can trace onto the muslin
- Pinking shears or rotary cutter with pinking blade
- One fine red marking pencil or pen
- One red fabric marker
- A sewing machine or needle and thread
- A frame with or without protective glass

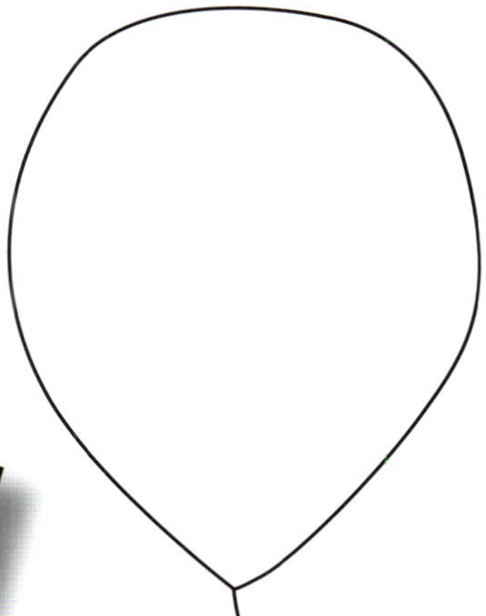

Using pinking shears, trim the edges of the quilted muslin piece into the size and shape you want for the finished project. Run a line of machine or hand stitching about a quarter inch from the outside of the entire piece to prevent fraying and to keep the batting from pulling out on the edges while the work is underway.

Trace the pattern from the book (or another source if you or your partner have a favorite image) and cut out a copy of the image. Trace it onto the muslin using a fine red marking pen or pencil.

When you're ready to sit down with your project partner, make sure you have a little redwork project to work on yourself, or are working on tracing another pattern for your partner, so that you are both working on something very similar.

Explain that redwork is outlining and have your partner trace over your red markings. Your partner may do a little coloring and may request more colors – that's fine! The point is that you two are working together to make something.

When your partner is done with the project, explain that we frame beautiful art and fit the piece in the frame. You may also display it as a wall hanging, without a frame or perhaps as a pillow.

Note:
Fabric markers are NOT washable, so be sure to outfit your partner in an old shirt to serve as an artist's smock, and protect your work surface with waxed or freezer paper.

Redwork templates

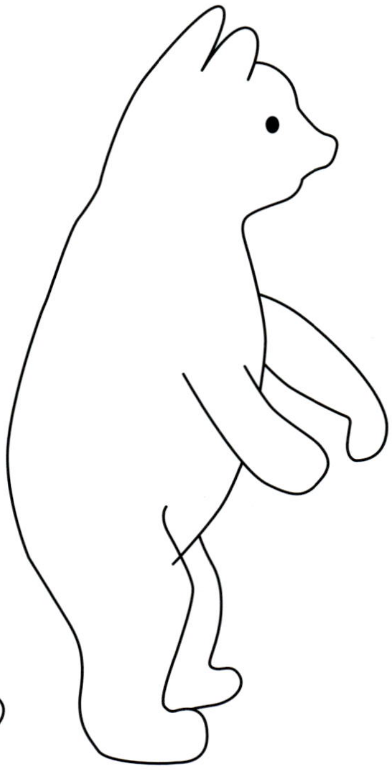